Mel Bay Presents

Uke Ballads
A Treasury of Twenty-Five Love Songs Old and New
Especially Arranged for the Romantic Ukulele

compiled, written
and produced
by Ian Whitcomb

CD CONTENTS

1	Beautiful Dreamer [2:40]	14	Blue Jeans (Dick Zimmerman, piano) [3:10]
2	Shine On Harvest Moon [1:46]	15	Homesick (Dick Zimmerman, piano) [2:34]
3	When I Lost You [2:45]	16	When We're Dancing (Randy Woltz, xylophone) [2:22]
4	Peg O' My Heart [1:32]	17	Dreams [2:18]
5	You Made Me Love You [3:26]	18	If You've Ever Loved (Randy Woltz, vibraphone) [2:20]
6	If I Had My Way [2:49]	19	I Just Knew (Regina Whitcomb, vocal; David Raksin, conductor) [3:24]
7	If We Can't Be The Same Old Sweethearts [3:07]	20	Paradise Island (Fred Sokolow, steel guitar) [3:24]
8	Smiles (Regina Whitcomb, vocal) [1:40]	21	In The Garden [2:57]
9	I Hate To Lose You [3:37]	22	My Dog Has Fleas (A Love Song) [2:08]
10	In The Land Of Beginning Again (David Pinto, piano) [2:08]	23	My Confession [2:13]
11	I'm Sorry I Made You Cry (Dick Zimmerman, piano) [2:33]	24	I Love You [2:09]
12	I'm Always Chasing Rainbows (David Pinto, piano) [2:12]	25	Goodnight [1:39]
13	I'm Forever Blowing Bubbles [1:44]		

The music on the companion compact disc is performed by Ian Whitcomb and his various bands and orchestras. Apart from vocals, Ian plays ukulele, tiple, banjolele, accordion, and piano. When there are vocalists and instrumental soloists other than Ian they are indicated. We are grateful to ITW Industries, Inc. for permission to use these recordings.

For a free catalog of Ian Whitcomb products (CDs, books, videos), write to ITW Industries at Box 451, Altadena, California, 91003. Or visit Ian's website at www.ianwhitcomb.com. Listen to Ian's radio show at www.radiofreeworld.com.

© 2001 BY MEL BAY PUBLICATIONS, INC., PACIFIC, MO 63069.
ALL RIGHTS RESERVED. INTERNATIONAL COPYRIGHT SECURED. B.M.I. MADE AND PRINTED IN U.S.A.
No part of this publication may be reproduced in whole or in part, or stored in a retrieval system, or transmitted in any form or by any means, electronic, mechanical, photocopy, recording, or otherwise, without written permission of the publisher.

Visit us on the Web at www.melbay.com — E-mail us at email@melbay.com

CONTENTS

Introduction 3
About The Author (And His Ukes) 10
Tuning 13

The Old Songs

Beautiful Dreamer (1865) 16
Shine On Harvest Moon (1909) 20
When I Lost You (1912) 24
Peg O' My Heart (1913) 28
You Made Me Love You (1913) 31
If I Had My Way (1913) 36
If We Can't Be The Same Old Sweethearts (Then We'll Just Be The Same Old Friends) (1913) 40
Smiles (1917) 44
I Hate To Lose You (I'm So Used To You Now) (1918) 46
In The Land Of Beginning Again (1918) 50
I'm Sorry I Made You Cry (1918) 54
I'm Always Chasing Rainbows (1918) 56
I'm Forever Blowing Bubbles (1919) 60
Blue Jeans (1920) 64
Homesick (1922) 68

The New Songs

When We're Dancing (2000) 74
Dreams (1999) 78
If You've Ever Loved (2000) 80
I Just Knew (1991) 82
Paradise Island (2000) 84
In The Garden (2000) 86
My Dog Has Fleas (A Love Song) (2000) 88
My Confession (1996) 90
I Love You (1999) 92
Goodnight (1981) 94

Other Books by Ian Whitcomb 96

Introduction

Coupling the lively little ukulele with the slow-moving big-hearted ballad might appear at first sight to be an unholy alliance. For the uke is associated with a bouncing outdoor merriment, while the ballad so often deals in darkened rooms where love on a sofa is the desire of the moment. But wait! One can handle the uke in such a way that gently murmuring strums emerge to act as a sweet stream of accompaniment upon which one's vocal croons can float along smoothly and pleasingly, like fragrant rose petals on a balmy afternoon.

I'm starting to burst rather flowery — I don't mean to overpower you with the musk of overblown Victorian parlor songs full of "thees" and "thous," of tragic maidens and lovelorn swains, of music that sticks in the mud.

There's only one Victorian number in this collection, *Beautiful Dreamer*, and it's way out on the sea and nicely salty-poetic. I've even sped it up to be uke-friendly and danceable. We're not in stiff collars here but in open-neck white shirts (not Hawaiian-patterned, though—this is mainland material), with our sleeves rolled up tastefully.

Ian Whitcomb

We're in that glorious first flush of Tin Pan Alley (circa 1900-1922), when the sentimental song, romantic and melancholy and dashingly direct, was put on wheels (whether as waltz or foxtrot) to compete with the frenetic energy of ragtime and then jazz. An Alleyman like "Ragtime" Jimmy Monaco knew that his customers needed time-out from turkey-trotting in order to ponder affairs of the heart (bursting, broken, or steadily beating as one). So, like any decent pro, he could swing easily from *At the Ragtime Ball* to *I'm Crying Just For You*. Indeed, his *You Made Me Love You* (the same year, 1913, as the above songs), started life as a raggy piece *I Didn't Want to Do It! I Didn't Want to Do It!* but was slowed into the guilt-ridden wail of a seductee by none other than the king of over-excitedness, Al Jolson.

Of course, it was Irving Berlin who, in the teen years of the 20th Century, was reckoned to be the pastmaster of the pop song in all moods and rhythms. He'd become particularly good at sob stuff. By the late 1920s he'd become so adept at self-pity *(All Alone, All By Myself, How About Me?,* etc.), that one of his songwriter colleagues opined: "The guy lugs a portable wailing wall around with him !". However, it was as a writer of artless ethnic comedy material as well as ragtime anthems that Berlin had made his name back in the 1910s and just before. Not until the death of his first wife Dorothy (of typhoid fever caught during their 1912 honeymoon in Cuba) inspired him to pour his grief into a waltz vessel, did he come up with a winning ballad. *When I Lost You* has a well-wrought melody set to nice juicy harmonies—a perfect marriage of naked sentiment to a sentimental showcase: the old-fashioned waltz, staple of the lachrymose 1890s.

This triumphant mix of art and commerce is the formula for all the other classic sentimental songs to be found in *Uke Ballads*. They've survived (or I've revived them, in some cases) because they're all heartfelt, however artless, reaching out to touch you to the core, providing you're willing and not some jaded sophisticate with an overlong cigarette holder and a permanently raised eyebrow.

I know you couldn't possibly be one of those types because you're reading this book, but I'm sure you know who I'm banging on about—the people who call this material corny.

I'll admit that some of the songs aren't exactly evergreens but I can assure you that when I perform them at concerts and festivals and even dank night clubs, folks approach me afterwards to inquire whether there's a recording available. And I'm always happy to oblige, knowing I've not only made someone happy to be sad but also gotten the cash to buy me and my wife a slap-up dinner.

How well I remember introducing *In The Land Of Beginning Again* during a typically raucous Dixieland festival at some faceless hotel too close to L. A. airport. Stationed beside a swimming pool full of screaming, splashing kids, competing with the blare of Bill Bailey brass from nearby, I soldiered on, just me and Ukie, with this beautiful ballad of reconciliation. As my last plunk faded so an old fellow approached me and, with a tear in his eye and a break in his voice, told me how much better he felt and asked for the title. The following year, at the same hellish venue, his widow requested the same song: "You know, it guided him through those last days," she said. Such is the power of popular song: it can "make you feel a thought," as songwriter E.Y.Harburg *Over The Rainbow* succinctly said. A sturdy ballad can warm us hearth-like, taking us through unwanted winters of our life so long as we keep performing, whether with full-blown orchestra or simply a mutter on a solitary walk.

All of the classic ballads here were published before the ukulele established itself as an instrument to be taken seriously by the pop industry, before it became the 1920s equivalent of the rock guitar.

The ukulele had entered western consciousness in 1879 when several of these baby guitars, called "braguinha" by their Portuguese makers, arrived in Hawaii on a ship. The locals, especially their royalty, took an instant liking to the chirpy-cheerful sound and were soon strumming, picking, and composing on what they now called "ukulele," meaning "jumping flea." Not very romantic, really, when translated. It's often better not to get translations when dealing with foreign languages. Hawaiian is most mellifluous, especially if you don't know what it means, and therefore, like French, is best left alone. Not until the Pan-Pacific International Exposition in San Francisco in 1915 was the mainland exposed to the sweetness and light of Hawaiian music with its ukes and, of course, its roller-coaster steel guitars. Tin Pan Alley responded to the native hit of the festival, *On The Beach At Waikiki,* with a barrage of comedy stuff like *They're Wearing 'Em Higher In Hawaii* and *Yaaka Hula Hickey Dula.* As yet, there's no lovey-doviness attached to the islands, just novelty value.

But by 1926 ukuleles were taking hold as the instrument of choice for the young set — the jazz babies and their beaus: the Martin guitar company produced 14,101 ukes in that year alone. And by now every piece of pop sheet music contained a uke chord diagram above the melody line to show you where to put your fingers when the harmony changed. Why, it was possible to reduce even Wagner to four string fundamentals. No room for pretentiousness in the world of ukery! Chord grids lasted right up into the early years of rock & roll. Then rock conquered, making the uke appear childish and uncool, and so, like the accordion, it was banished to the closet.
What a pity that the uke hadn't yet caught on in the early years of the century, when Tin Pan Alley, as we have seen, was producing simple songs with four-square barbershop harmonies, as yet unclogged by clever-clever jazz chords. For the uke would have been the perfect fellow conspirator for a young man out serenading at night, with hopes for a rosy future or merely flirtation underneath the arbors.

What a pity, too, that when the uke became prominent in the Jazz Age it was as a trendy prop, like the hip flask, the raccoon coat, the tin of rouge, the megaphone. Ukes were for accompanying the likes of *Five Foot Two* and "Vo-Do-De-O." This unfortunate lingering association has led many to believe that the instrument is only good for a laugh, for conveying high-speed frivolity and silliness, when, in truth, the uke can issue a plangency like nothing on earth, helping lovers beneath a harvest moon to attain that loving they haven't had since April, January, June or July. And the uke's essential jauntiness can dry up some of the dripping self-pity of *I'm Always Chasing Rainbows* and *I'm Forever Blowing Bubbles.* A cleanly moving strum can work wonders, even in waltztime.

Speaking of strums, we can now introduce the legacy of Travellin' Jack Strum, a fellow who should be dragged out of the shadows of history. In my songbook, *Ukulele Heaven* (Mel Bay Publications, 1999), I reproduced most of a memoir I'd discovered behind an iron door in the basement of The Huntington Library, San Marino, California. I do my research at this library; they have lent me a desk in a quiet and cozy corner beneath a little-used staircase. The memoir was written by one Irving Fisher, founder of a ukulele vaudeville act called "Murray's Mainlanders" who'd achieved a certain measure of success on the West Coast of the early 1920s, mainly by intelligent use of a chorus line of grass-skirted girlies with special skills in the movement of both uke and hips.

What I'd omitted from the memoir was Fisher's tirade against a rival uke entertainer called Travellin' Jack Strum. Entertaining enough stuff, but it held up my story. However, now that we're mingling strums and sentiment this is the time to quote Irving on Jack because the memoir throws light on the potency of uke balladry in skillful, if devilish, hands....................

Strum, like so many of the adventurers found scurrying around Southern California in those days, was a self-invented creature. His real name was Samuel Widgerly and he'd been born in Croydon, a rather dull town, in the England of the late 19th century. Both his name and his birthplace indicate that he was not from the top shelf. Not quite common as muck but from that dangerous and resourceful class known as the lower-middle. Neither one thing nor the other — watch out for these people!

Widgerly, having failed as a salesman of shoes and pianos, respectively, sailed to San Francisco in 1915 just in time to avoid being conscripted into the Great War. Here, like Irving Fisher, he was exposed to the delights and potential of the ukulele as demonstrated by the Hawaiian ensembles performing at their own national pavilion during the Panama-Pacific International Exposition. After some chatting up of a clutch of hula girls he zeroed in on a Mr. Leon Nunes, self-styled "inventor" of the ukulele, in the process pushing aside Irving Fisher (who'd been conversing with Nunes) and immediately winning the attention of the inventor due to the pleasant sound of his voice and accent. "You trill like a sweet bird of paradise," said Nunes. "You are goody-goody." This made Irving stamp off in a real tizzy, thus missing his chance to be presented with a Nunes uke (at a reasonable price). Widgerly gladly coughed up the cash for the instrument.

Rather than tread the boards of vaudeville like Irving and his Mainlanders, Widgerly concentrated on the private sector: he hit the homes of the idle rich, wangling his way into drawing room (and even boudoir) via the costume of a romantic troubadour of the open road and, of course, that accent and voice which had so enchanted Mr. Nunes. Fake British aristocrat, of course, and now billed as "Travellin' Jack Strum," like a disguised prince in a ruritanian romance. But the concoction made for a striking picture: broad cowboy hat, trailing bandana of silk against a bright plaid open neck shirt, tight corduroy trousers emphasizing a bursting virility. He certainly made it over Irving and company as a talking point with the wealthy women of a certain age.

So while the Mainlanders were sweating it out in some seedy vaudeville theatre in downtown Los Angeles, Travellin' Jack was beguiling the high society of Pasadena and environs with sweet ballads trilled to the accompaniment of his Nunes ukulele. (Fisher had a Martin). So jealous did Fisher become that he took to employing waiters and the odd butler to deliver reports of Strum's activities at these mansion functions. There may have been a little sexual jealousy involved because Irving was not a handsome man while Strum was decidedly attractive, well-built, with thick tousled curly blond hair and large sensuous lips. The ladies of flower garden, luncheon, and Bridge, fell for him in droves, and as cocktail hour passed into dinner time so they waxed more romantic about this travellin' man and his instrument, while their menfolk, captains of big business, cleared their throats but put up with this silly business for the sake of domestic calm.

Ian Whitcomb

Here's a particularly virulent passage from the Irving Fisher memoir:

My spies tell me that the Strum was at his worst—or at his best, according to his morals—last night during a dinner party of Mrs. Garrington-Linke's up on St. Michael's Mount in Pasadena. The occasion was a party held after the annual Midsummer Night's Dream rose-arranging competition and the ladies were flushed with too much sherry wine and deep into the giggle stage. I'm reliably informed that the wretch Strum made an appearance from the pool house with a gilded robe thrown around his shoulders which he quickly proceeded to shrug off revealing a sort of neoclassical Greek bathing slip. The bastard is so well-equipped that this exhibition made the ladies gasp and thrill while their husbands resorted to commenting favorably on the "poetic and Praxitelian pose" and other garbage they've no doubt learned from too many evenings around those statues that stud Henry Huntington's mansion.

Next thing, pulling out his uke from behind his back, he launched into Peg O' My Heart, *holding the instrument low, just in front of his groin — a gross misuse of our precious ukulele—and nancying the lyrics to the women as if to each one individually. He followed up with* You Made Me Love You, *a doggone dangerous number in the hands of a lounge lizard like Strum who can make it sound like he's a victim of a woman's hypnotic sex appeal, as if, godammit, the guy's been raped. You always have to be careful when handling hearts, but in this case Strum was aiming lower, at the purely sensual, at flesh and the making of roaring blood. Why the husbands didn't protest is beyond me. Maybe they'd been liquored into complacency or maybe they were just plain tuckered out after a hard day at the office.*

Later — much later so I'm told by the waiter I hired, who'd shimmied up a drainpipe to watch Strum from a narrow balustrade outside an upper window — the lavender lover had actually wormed his way into Mrs. Garrington-Linke's boudoir for, supposedly, a nightcap with madam and some of her closer friends, there to work his sorcery in a world of face cream jars and corsets and such. At this witching hour he brought out his secret weapon: a new kind of vocal technique, the merest whisper, like a mother crooning to her babies, only in this case these were mighty aged babes and plenty in need of a good pressing. Well, my waiter told me the "nightcap" turned into a romp with pillows and nightgowns, etc. I could go on for volumes but I'll simply drag a veil over this bedroom farce. My point is this: Strum has deflowered our instrument and our music; he has debased our coinage. I wonder how much he made for that nights gig? I must ask my spies.

Who could have guessed that our dear little uke could be duped into becoming a collaborator in a scene causing so much ire? But these were early days in the history of sweet music when experiments were allowed, when cowboys like Strum could ride their peculiar range. This was before the uke was tamed and made safe for domestic usage, before gentlemen like Cliff Edwards and Johnny Marvin, both homely, had established themselves as purveyors of non-threatening balladry. In the 1930s appeared the saucy George Formby, with his toothy grin and seaside jollity. In the 1950s all would be settled and sedate thanks to the avuncular personality of Arthur Godfrey. And in the 1960s the Age of Camp would produce Tiny Tim, shortly after I'd made a stab at resurrecting the uke with my (sort of) hit recording of 1916's "Where Did Robinson Crusoe Go With Friday On Saturday Night?" Everything was sweetness and light, novelty and laughter.

The dangerous days of Travellin' Jack Strum had been lost in time, were not even history until I discovered Irving Fisher's memoir in the far recesses of the Huntington Library and learned of that thrilling happening at Mrs. Garrington-Linke's party back in 1923.

Carrying On The Grand Tradition

Although I spend an awful lot of time delving around in the past, doing my best to bring it back alive, I also try to add to the library of old-fashioned pop songs by writing my own. This isn't only due to self-obsession and a desire for immortality: it's also because I need new material for my appearances and sometimes my requirements aren't met by what's available from the treasury.

For example, *Goodnight* was written as a finale to my act at the Mayfair Music Hall in Santa Monica when I was a regular on the bill during the 1970s. I can't improve on what I wrote about the song in my first Mel Bay songbook, *Treasures Of Tin Pan Alley* (published in 1995 and now out-of-print, but you can get copies from my garage if you write):

I always liked British Music Hall comedians who, after spending their entire act reeling off jokes, would end with a sentimental, often reflective, song like Isn't It Grand To See Someone Smile? *or* Friends And Neighbors.

Goodnight *is in this tradition — a thank-you to the audience for tolerating me; a hope that you'll miss me; and a suggestion that song can break the wall of darkness, conquering oblivion. Music has a tendency to go abstract; language can tell it straight and human. Put the two together properly and you have a joy forever. That's why I love popular songs!*

I Just Knew is my attempt at adding a felt love song to my repertoire. Like Irving Berlin inspecting his sheet music warehouse and, noticing a paucity of waltzes, immediately knocking out a few, I supplied my need for a ballad expressing an understanding of a loved one who simply can't say, "I love you." Perhaps I had my own emotional limitations in mind. At any rate, audiences for years had been encouraging me to stick to my comic numbers such as *Wurzel Fudge — The Village Idiot*. Let them hear my other side, let them see that I can write a romantic number for a woman to sing—in this case, my wife. Perhaps the number is a little self-serving but the tune is catchy and the situation not entirely unknown. As I wrote about *I Just Knew* in *Treasures Of Tin Pan Alley*:

Luckily, the girl understands The Great Unstated, and anyway she's had enough of silver-tongued lovers spewing stuff they never meant.

Our recording, with my wife Regina singing with an orchestra conducted by the noted movie composer and songwriter David Raksin, is from the CD of my 1992 musical comedy, *LotusLand*.

In a way, *Dreams* and *I Love You* were written-to-order. I had been invited to contribute songs for an independent movie project called *Stanley's Gig*, a story concerning a ukulele entertainer at an old folks home. The picture is now completed and stars William Sanderson and Faye Dunaway, with me in the cameo role of Smiling Jack, a radio uke personality.

Rather than have the producers have to face the usual exorbitant dollar demand for world licensing of an old chestnut like *Let Me Call You Sweetheart* (the song had already been written into the screenplay by the unknowing writer), I offered to come up with a bunch of new "old" numbers within a day or so. Banging away at the mini-piano in our drawing room I completed both *Dreams* and *I Love You* in one afternoon. Whenever I got stuck I called on the spirit of Irving Berlin to please come and help me out. I would ask myself: "How would Irving have approached this problem?"

Dreams has an echo of the sentimental songs I remember from end-of-pier shows in the rainy England of the late 1940s, that age of austerity when we longed to be in a brighter, dryer place. I must have been thinking of the America I'd seen on the screen. I'm happy to inform you that an entertainer called The Uke Lady of Brooklyn has downloaded *Dreams* from off the World Wide Web and now performs it at hospitals in the New York area.

The waltz, *I Love You*, didn't fit the requirements of "Stanley's Gig" (scripts keep changing in movieland) but the producers asked me if I had a slow, smoochy number for a flashback scene set in a black nightclub of the 1940s in which a sexy young woman croons jazzily and so mesmerically that men start walking towards her in a state of ecstasy. Had I got such a number? You bet I had! And I performed the little pastiche waltz as a smoldering ballad in 4/4 time. It worked the trick perfectly and, even better, now that the melody was stretched, the jazz singer (Marla Gibbs) could decorate each note and, in the great gaps between each phrase, the accompanying musicians could insert those improvised response phrases they so adore and which, so I'm told, constitute a great part of that mysterious art called jazz.

The music to *When We're Dancing* was created in a very practical manner. In the late summer of 2000 Regina was teaching a vintage dance class in a Pasadena church hall. I was providing live piano music and when she reached the Fox Trot of 1914 — the original bouncy one and not the sleeker step that took over in the 1920s — I improvised a stately but relaxed sort of jog trot.

The tune haunted me with its sinuous and insinuating chromatics. Like onion rings and pecan pies, like everything that gives me guilty pleasure, I wanted it constantly. Well, one shouldn't throw away a possible commercial melody so, a little later, around "Jeopardy" time, I sat down at my desk and started in on some lyrics, letting my subconscious have a say in the proceedings. What happens when we're dancing? A sad story started to act itself out: she never holds him close no matter what dance step they're doing; surely she has another man on her mind but who can it be? Why, it's the man he once was years ago when they were younger and happier! Where does this stuff come from? God only knows.

Next I played the finished chorus — the standard 32 bars that's a dance requirement — to my piano pedagogue. He pronounced it "charming" and said we'd make the song our class exercise by writing it out on paper and he'd be back in a few minutes with manuscript and pencils. While he was gone I sat at his great monster of a Steinway and, inspired by masters not necessarily from Tin Pan Alley, I composed a verse using weird minor chords with flatted fifths, chords dependent on exactly the right bass note. But never mind: the uke stands for no such complexity, seeing it as obfuscation, and so, in the book, you can finger perfectly acceptable stripped-down versions of these chords with just two stops, as you'll see. When my teacher returned I played him the verse and he was delighted to hear what I'd snatched from a little exposure to Schubert, Chopin, and Bartok. "Steal without conscience," he advised me. "Art knows no morals."

Under his guidance I wrote *In The Garden,* not a pleasant sight. A simple enough melody, almost country style, until the middle part (or "release" as the pros like to call it) where it suddenly turns edgy and even jagged, with a little help from Bartok. Later I added the words and it was here again that my dark side took over, leading me from a sunny garden setting into the depths of despair. "You write such nice tunes," said Regina. "Why do you have to then go and nasty them up with your words?"

Like *In The Garden,* my other songs in this collection serve no real purpose other than simply existing. They weren't written with movies, musicals, or dances, in mind. *If You've Ever Loved* evolved one evening at home when there was nothing on television and I was at the mini-piano rolling around some rich and fruity minor sevenths with flatted fifths and that crucial bass note. I wanted to see where this particular A min7/flat 5, would take me, this exotic, this almost erotic chord. Not wanting to be led too far astray, to be taken into a forbidden land, I tethered my chord to a bass note that moved correctly in the true blue circle of fifths: A-D-G-C-F-B♭ (home at last!). I approximated a latin rhythm — a rhumba, I believe — and then the words started tumbling naturally from the old reliable subconscious and that equally reliable chest of good-sounding words. Again, no need to worry about the missing bass notes in your uke chordings. A bass player can supply your anchor. And anyway, I prefer to hear the uke in the context of a small string band.

My Dog Has Fleas starts with a musical phrase of fundamental ukery. How that tune-up tune has irritated me in the past! How I've wanted to strike out at jeering jazzers when they've called out, "My dog has fleas!", as I've been clambering onto the bandstand! Therefore recently I decided to sleep with the enemy. I grabbed the offensive tune and forced it into a song structure, letting the flea situation ease into a hymn of man/dog devotion. We've had three dogs since I moved to the Altadena house in 1979: Beefy was celebrated in an instrumental, Inspector was memorialized in a rather tearful goodbye song (published in *Ukulele Heaven*). *My Dog Has Fleas* is about a living animal, our latest dog, a puppy called Rollo. Or Rollo H. Danks when he's been bad. He was found, as a newly born, wandering the roads of a ranch area called Shadow Hills, apparently abandoned. He has no pedigree; everyone has their own theories as to what breed he is. But he's the love of our life and he looks like he needs a saddle.

Paradise Island is an afterthought, written just days before the final recording session when I thought I had a full complement of songs. But, inspired by the fact that we'd be recording at a studio run by Rick Cunha, a fine

a full complement of songs. But, inspired by the fact that we'd be recording at a studio run by Rick Cunha, a fine ukulele player and the grandson of the legendary Sonny Cunha, who was writing Hawaiian songs in the ragtime era and who is the credited arranger on *On The Beach At Waikiki,* I sat down and tried to capture the quintessence of faraway places. This was in early December, 2000, during those tumultuous days when courts were fighting over the claims of would-be Presidents, and I suppose I was reacting by turning back my thoughts to childhood and a seemingly simpler time—the summer of 1946 on the East coast of England.

I was five and rushing down to the lake by the sea to compete in a rowing race at the annual regatta. As I approached the boathouse I was halted suddenly by ethereal music pouring from bullhorn speakers up in the trees. It was my first experience of the gulp-provoking swoop and glide of the steel guitar and the cheery plunk of the ukulele. I was transported to a paradise that I have been trying to find ever since. This was when the world was still bleeding from the recent war and when there were strange and deadly objects still lurking in the bulrushes of that little lake we called "The Meare."

Now I realize that the music I'd heard over those Tannoy speakers was most likely a record made locally by one Felix Mendelssohn (a descendant of the great classical composer) and his Hawaiian Serenaders, most of whom had never set foot in any tropical island and probably would have dearly loved to find respite from the rain and the ration book. But the music they made was, and is still, as decent as any from Hawaii itself. This 1946 elixir of a few minutes was enough to win me to Hawaiian sounds for life. Rock 'n' roll and rhythm & blues may have diverted me during my teens and twenties but now, as sunset approaches, I find myself returning to that siren music from the bullhorns near the lake.

So , *Paradise Island* is my attempt to stir up a potion capable of returning me to a certain good old feeling. A sort of drug, but one with spiritual front effects, I hope: on this island God's deal is done for us; what that deal turns out to be depends on how we've behaved on the mainland.

Finally, *My Confession* is a song of thanks to my wife Regina, who combines all that's worthwhile but doesn't let you take it for granted. She has lodged a complaint about the lyrics: "I am not, and never have been, your mother!". Nevertheless, I would like people to sing this song freely.

ABOUT THE AUTHOR
(AND HIS UKES)

Ian Whitcomb, born in England in 1941, has been singing pop songs since childhood. At prep school he ran a lavatory paper-and-comb band, performing hits of the day like *That Doggie In The Window*; at public school, in his teens, he played tea chest bass in the jazz band and rhythm guitar in the skiffle group. And, of course, he sang, whether it be *St. James Infirmary* or *Sportin' Life*. One day, during the holidays, he discovered an almost toy-like ukulele at his cousin's house and he worked out some simple chords to an index finger strum. An all-round left-hander, Ian never bothered to reverse the strings and never has to this day. Thus, he is self-taught and the result is that some of his chord shapes are unique, including an odd use of the thumb. There's nobody who sounds quite like him; conversely, he can't duplicate the syncopated strums of his heroes George Formby and Cliff ("Ukulele Ike" Edwards). Over and over again, he listened to their records of the 1920s and 1930s as the 1950s turned into the 1960s. He bought a cheap local uke. He learned to amuse his friends on long car journeys until they'd had quite enough. And then he'd sing to himself, for succor and for solace.

Meanwhile, his interest in a tiny instrument considered by many to be an irrelevant trifle didn't preclude him from taking part in the rock 'n' roll revolution. He relished Bill Haley and Elvis Presley. He wanted to find a way into their American dream. But who, in the great far country of big skies, could possibly be interested in an Englishman singing the blues?

Then, amazingly, the British Invasion came and the problem went away. Ian rolled in on a wave from Ireland: while studying modern history & political thought at Trinity College Dublin, he made some rock 'n' roll recordings which somehow got him into the American hit parade. One of them, a novelty panting track called *You Turn Me On* reached #8 in the "Billboard" chart of July, 1965.

Finding himself in the country of Elvis as a teen idol, he almost immediately torpedoed his chances of continuing to cause shrieks and sighs from both sexes by producing a Martin ukulele (bought in an L.A. pawnshop) and launching into antiques such as *Where Did Robinson Crusoe Go With Friday On Saturday Night?* To be fair, his *Tower* 45 rpm recording of this 1916 Al Jolson hit did manage to make the Top Twenty on the West

Coast in 1966; and, the same year, Ian could be seen brazenly strumming his uke as he sang a Beatles song on Dick Clark's *Where The Action Is!* to a seated circle of bemused kids. All of this happened before the coming of Tiny Tim.

By the end of the 1960s Ian had become disenchanted with rock — it seemed so pompous, so pretentious, so complainingly loud — and, in turn, the scenemakers no longer had a role for him. A faded One Hit Wonder, he was by now enamored of Tin Pan Alley and henceforth he dedicated himself to keeping alive the old flavors, not only because he was a historian and escapist, but also because his insides responded emotionally to the Alley's spirit of big-heartedness, sentimentality, simple music, lack of cynicism, bourbon and cigars. Taking the old song styles as his model he started crafting his own numbers, reflecting his own take on life. He abhorred campiness. However, as an entertainer, he sometimes lapsed into playing to the crowd — anything for a laugh — and he'd hate himself in the morning.

In 1967 the pawnshop Martin had been exchanged for a brand new model 3M Martin bought in Hollywood for several hundred dollars. He still performs and records with "Ukie," who still lives in the original hardshell case (now severely battered and almost totally naked to the wood). Over the years, especially during the difficult 70s and 80s, Ukie has suffered greatly, has been left on railway station platforms, in trains speeding away from Ian, in Missouri streets. Always he's returned. He's been bashed into stand mikes on stage, accused of being an automatic weapon, sat upon, cursed. Many times has he been repaired. And yet he survives to produce the sweetest, prettiest sounds, and to increasingly be called upon to accompany sentimental ballads. For Ian, as he moves gently into late middle age, feels more comfortable with slower, reflective, and considered, songs. He only performs frenzied novelties like *T'Ain't No Sin To Take Off Your Skin And Dance Around In Your Bones* when the crowd's roar becomes a command.

Today Ian is happy to be a part of The Great Ukulele Revival sweeping the world, spearheaded by "Jumpin' Jim" Beloff who, almost single-handedly, has applied his skills learned as a corporate executive (together with his enthusiasm for the uke) to place the instrument squarely back in the mainstream of entertainment. Jim is tireless, inspirational, and motivational. He would be great on the mashed potato & rubber chicken hotel convention circuit. His products pour out, almost overtaking Ian's output: he has published a beautiful coffee table book, *The Ukulele- A Visual History* (Miller-Freeman), a CD called *Legends Of Ukulele* (Rhino), plus lots of uke song theme books for his company Flea Market Music. And Ian is pleased as punch to be a part of these packages.

Jim (and his family) has also started manufacturing a very reasonably priced ukulele called a "Fluke." Triangular in shape and available in many colors and motifs (mine has a moon reflected over water), the Fluke sits securely on its bottom, so that, unlike "Ukie," he cannot so easily crash to the floor. My "Flukie" has been custom-made with a left-handed pickup so I can plug into an amplifier whenever I'm threatened on stage by electrified musicians. "Ukie," needless to say, is jealous but that's the way things must go if we're to stay relevant. You can hear both "Ukie" and "Flukie" strumming along in harmonious bipartisanship on several tracks of this book's companion CD (#3, 16, 18, 21, 22).

Fellow travelers in the Great Revival include George Harrison, Jimmy Buffett, and Lyle Ritz. All are Fluke owners. Todd Rundgren has been seen playing a uke. Pearl Jam feature one on a new recording. The Ukulele Orchestra Of Great Britain continue to widen the repertoire with their versions of Schubert works and Charlie Parker flights of fancy, even as The George Formby Society mass in their hundreds for *When I'm Cleaning Windows*. Here in Southern California we still celebrate "Uketopia" concerts at McCabe's Guitar Shop in Santa Monica. Recently a TV crew recorded us for posterity and, possibly, money. Among the artistes in that show was Janet Klein, as pretty a period picture as you could imagine, and I'm proud to say that Ukie and I are now a permanent member of her backing group, The Parlor Boys. Catch us sometime. In a new movie called *The Cat's Meow*, Kursten Dunst sings to accompaniment by Ukie.

All over the globe countless multitudes are hourly joining the revolution, coming out of closets with ukes that had been hidden away in shame when the storm troopers of rock marched in. But now, as the skies clear, we can return like the prodigal son to our old folkways, unsullied by faddish cynics, and gaily join a never-ending snakeline of strummers and pickers spreading happiness by way of a certain pleasing plangency.

Ian Whitcomb on Dick Clark's *Where The Action Is,* shot near Malibu Beach in July, 1966. He was pioneering the ukulele in the Age of Rock.

Tuning

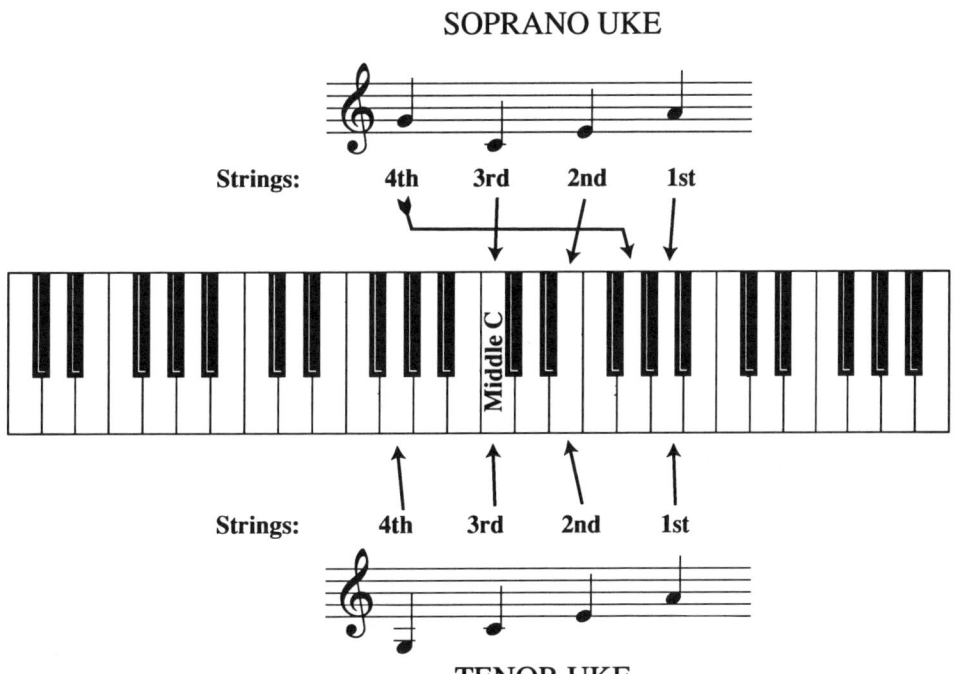

The Old Songs

Beautiful Dreamer

Words and Music by
Stephen Foster

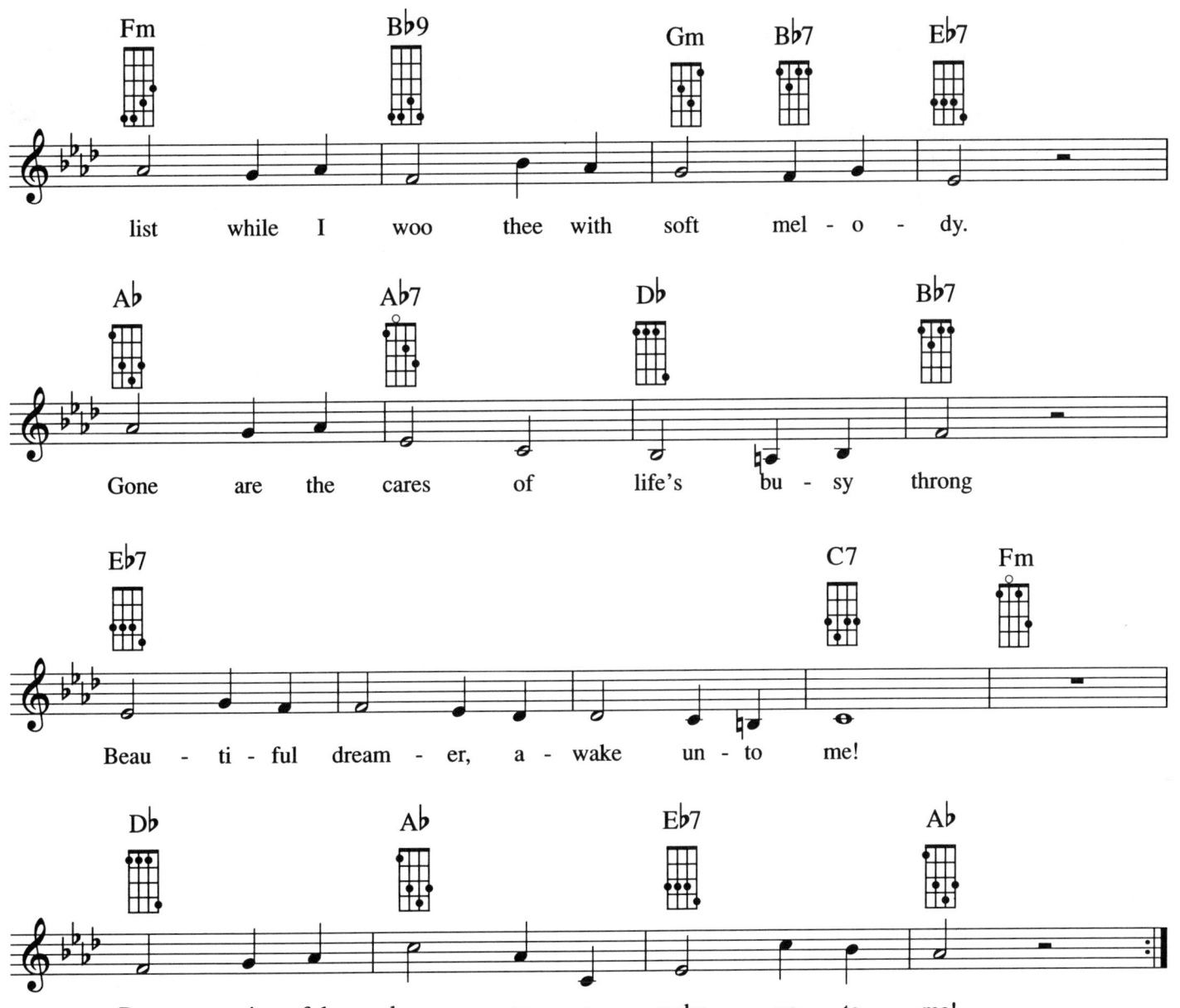

1. Beautiful dreamer, wake unto me,
   Starlight and dewdrops are waiting for thee,
   Sounds of the rude world heard in the day,
   Lulled by the moonlight have all pass'd away.
   Beautiful dreamer, queen of my song,
   List while I woo thee with soft melody.
   Gone are the cares of life's busy throng
   Beautiful dreamer, awake unto me!
   Beautiful dreamer, awake unto me!

2. Beautiful dreamer, out on the sea
   Mermaids are chanting the wild lorelie
   Over the streamlet vapors are borne,
   Waiting to fade at the bright coming moon.
   Beautiful dreamer, beam on my heart,
   E'en as the moon on the streamlet and sea,
   Then will all clouds of sorrow depart,
   Beautiful dreamer, awake unto me!
   Beautiful dreamer, awake unto me!

Shine On, Harvest Moon

Words by
Jack Norworth

Music by
Nora Bayes and Jack Norworth

Night was might-y dark so you could hard-ly see, For the moon re-fused to shine, Cou-ple sit-ting un-der-neath a wil-low tree,___ For love they pine,_____ Lit-tle maid was kind a-fraid of dark-ness So she said,___ "I guess I'll go," Boy be-gan to sigh, Looked up at the sky, Told the moon his lit-tle tale of woe.___

1. Night was mighty dark so you could hardly see,
   For the moon refused to shine,
   Couple sitting underneath a willow tree,
   For love they pine,
   Little maid was kind o' 'fraid of darkness
   So she said, "I guess I'll go,"
   Boy began to sigh, Looked up at the sky,
   Told the moon his little tale of woe.

2. I can't see why the boy should sigh,
   When by his side is the girl he loves so true,
   All he has to say is
   "Won't you be my bride,
   For I love you, why should I be telling you this secret
   When I know that you can guess,"
   Harvest moon will smile, shine on all the while,
   If the little girl should answer "Yes."

CHORUS: Oh, shine on, shine on harvest moon, up in the sky.
I ain't had no lovin' Since January, February, June or July,
Snow time ain't no time to stay outdoors and spoon,
So, shine on, shine on, harvest moon,
For me and my gal.

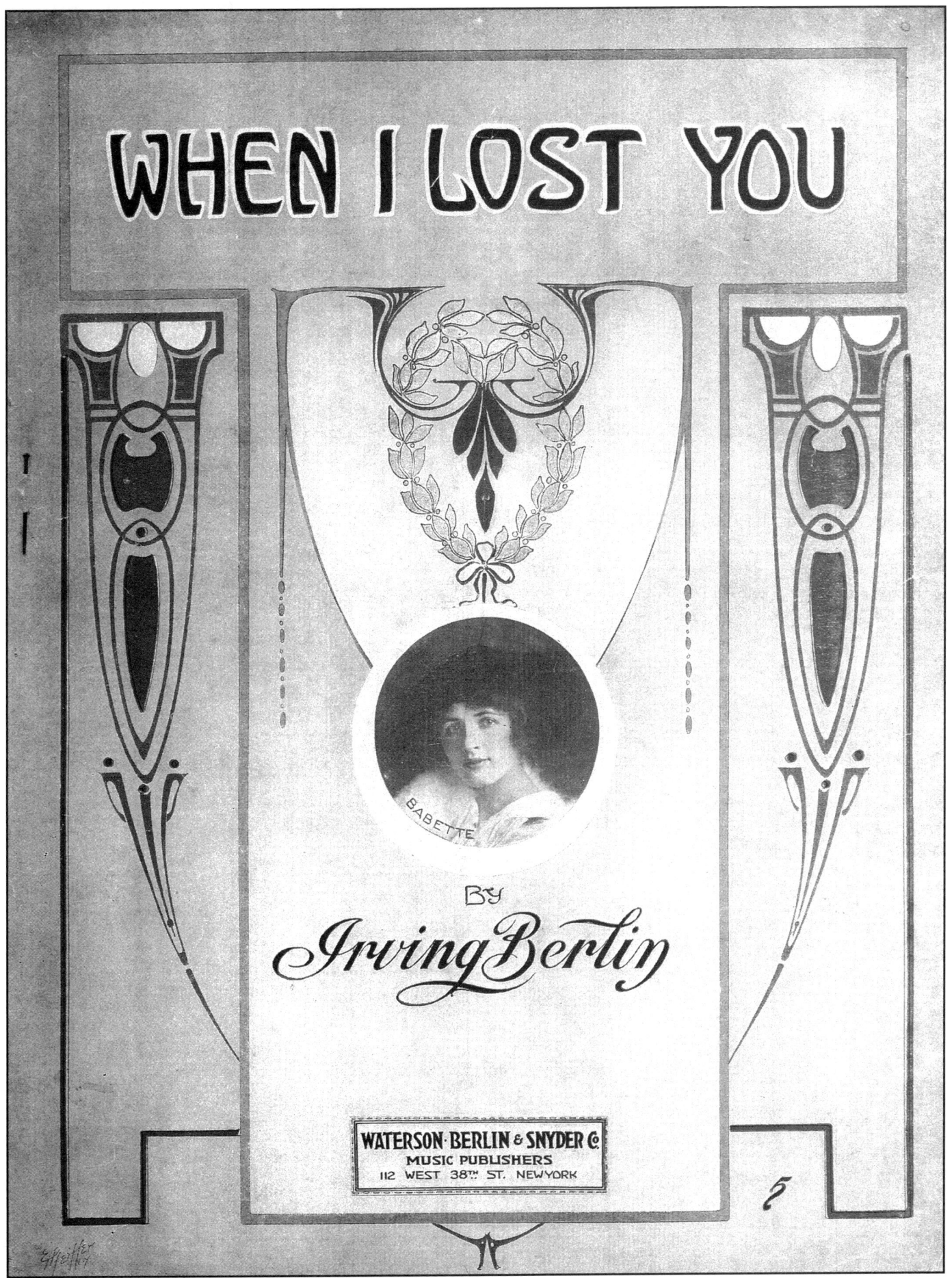

When I Lost You

1. The roses each one met with the sun,
   Sweetheart, when I met you. The sunshine had fled,
   The roses were dead, Sweetheart, when I lost you.

2. The birds ceased their song, right turned to wrong,
   Sweetheart, when I lost you. A day turned to years,
   The world seem'd in tears, Sweetheart, when I lost you.

CHORUS: I lost the sunshine and roses, I lost the heavens of blue.
I lost the beautiful rainbow, I lost the morning dew.
I lost the angel who gave me summer, the whole winter through,
I lost the gladness that turned into sadness, When I lost you.

Peg O' My Heart

Words by Alfred Bryan

Music by Fred Fischer

1. Oh! my heart's in a whirl, over one little girl,
   I love her, I love her, yes I do,
   Altho' her heart is far away,
   I hope to make her mine some day.
   Ev'ry beautiful rose, ev'ry violet knows,
   I love her, I love her fond and true,
   And her heart fondly sighs, as I sing to her eyes,
   Her eyes of blue, sweet eyes of blue, my darling!

2. When your heart's full of fears, and your eye full of tears,
   I'll kiss them, I'll kiss them all away,
   For, like the gold that's in your hair,
   Is all the love for you I bear. O, believe in me, do,
   I'm as lonesome as you, I miss you, I miss you all the day,
   Let the light of love shine,
   from your eyes into mine, and shine for aye,
   Sweetheart for aye, my darling!

CHORUS: Peg O' My Heart, I love you, we'll never part,
I love you, dear little girl, sweet little girl,
Sweeter than the rose of Erin, are your winning smiles endearin',
Peg O' My Heart, your glances with Irish art entrance us,
Come, be my own, come, make your home in my heart.

1. I've been worried all day long,
   Don't know if I'm right or wrong.
   I can't help just what I say,
   Your love makes me speak this way,
   Why, oh! why should I feel blue,
   Once I used to laugh at you,
   But now I'm crying, no use denying,
   There's no one else but you will do,

2. I had pictured in my mind,
   Some day I would surely find,
   Someone handsome, someone true,
   But I never thought of you,
   Now my dream of love is o'er,
   I want you and nothing more,
   Come on, enfold me, come on and hold me
   Just like you never did before,

CHORUS:

You made me love you,
I didn't want to do it,
I didn't want to do it,
You made me want you,
And all the time you knew it,
I guess you always knew it,
You made me happy sometimes
You made me glad,
But there were times dear,

You made me feel so bad.
You made me sigh for
I didn't want to tell you
I didn't want to tell you
I want some love that's true,
Yes, I do, 'deed I do, you know I do.
Give me, give me, what I cry for,
You know you got the brand of kisses that I'd die for.
You know you made me love you.

1. I'd like to make your golden dreams come true, dear,
   If I only had my way,
   A paradise this world would seem to you, dear,
   If I only had my way.

2. You'd never know a care, a pain, or sorrow,
   If I only had my way,
   I'd fill your cup of happiness tomorrow,
   If I only had my way.

CHORUS: If I had my way, dear,
Forever there'd be a garden of roses for you and for me,
A thousand and one things, dear,
I would do, just for you, just for you, just for you.
If I had my way we would never grow old,
And sunshine I'd bring ev'ry day,
You would reign all alone, like a queen on a throne
If I had my way.

If We Can't Be the Same Old Sweethearts, We'll Just Be the Same Old Friends

Words by Joe McCarthy
Music by Jimmie V. Monaco

Once we were sweet-hearts, Not so long a-go, Then I loved you so, But you did-n't know; You could-n't learn to love me, You're not to blame, But I like you just the same;

CHORUS (slow swing)

If we can't be the same old sweet-hearts, Then we'll just be the same old friends, For I want some-one like you, Just to tell my troub-les to, My

1. Once we were sweethearts, not so long ago,
   Then I loved you so, but you didn't know;
   You couldn't learn to love me, you're not to blame,
   But I like you just the same;

2. You said you loved me, not so long ago,
   But you didn't know, sweethearts come and go,
   Some day you'll love another, and later on,
   You may want me, when he's gone;

CHORUS: If we can't be the same old sweethearts,
Then we'll just be the same old friends,
For I want someone like you,
Just to tell my troubles to,
My happiness on you it all depends;
For I've known you too long to forget you,
And my old dream of love never ends,
Tho' I know you can't be mine,
We will meet from time to time,
And we'll just be the same old friends.

Smiles

Words by
J. Will Callahan

Music by
Lee S. Roberts

1. Dearie, now I know just what makes me love you so,
   Just what holds me and enfolds me in its golden glow;
   Dearie, now I see 'tis each smile so bright and free,
   For life's sadness turns to gladness, when you smile on me.

2. Dearie, when you smile ev'ry thing in life's worth while,
   Love grows fonder as we wander down each magic mile;
   Cheery melodies seem to float upon the breeze,
   Doves are cooing while they're wooing in the leafy trees.

CHORUS: There are smiles that makes us happy,
There are smiles that makes us blue,
There are smiles that steal away the teardrops.
As the sunbeams steal away dew,
There are smiles that have a tender meaning
That the eyes of love alone may see,
And the smiles that fill my life with sunshine
Are the smiles that you give to me.

1. We were so happy, you and I,
   But now I feel I could die;
   You changed your mind and said "goodbye,"
   And didn't tell me why.
   If you had left me years ago,
   It wouldn't hurt me so.

2. I learned the sweetness of your kiss,
   And now you make me feel like this;
   That isn't all I'm goin' to miss,
   A perfect world of bliss.
   Maybe you'll love someone some day,
   And love enough to say:

CHORUS: I hate to lose you, I'm used to you now, still I excuse you, for breaking your vow;
Just like the sunlight I found, I'm used to having you 'round;
You're all I've ever been thinking of, who am I goin' to love,
Now that you've turned me down? Just like the rose, dear,
That's used to the sun; its petals close, dear, when summer is done.
And I'm so used to your kisses, all the others seem strange;
Used to your lovin' and I don't want to change,
I hate to lose you, I'm so used to you now.

1. Sometimes there're tears behind a sunny smile,
   Some hearts hold sorrow for a long, long while,
   If we could only forget,
   Think how much further we'd get.
   And though our hearts are filled with sadness,
   We'll see the sunshine yet.

2. Don't ever feel that ev'ry hope is gone,
   It's always darkest just before dawn,
   Just try a smile through the tears,
   Some day you'll laugh at your fears.
   And though your life is filled with shadows,
   They'll fade through future years.

CHORUS: There's a land of beginning again,
Where skies are always blue,
Tho' we've made mistakes, that's true,
Let's forget the past and start life anew,
Tho' we've wandered by a river of tears,
Where sunshine won't come through;
Let's find that Paradise where sorrow can't live,
And learn the teachings of forget and forgive,
In the land of beginning again,
Where broken dreams come true.

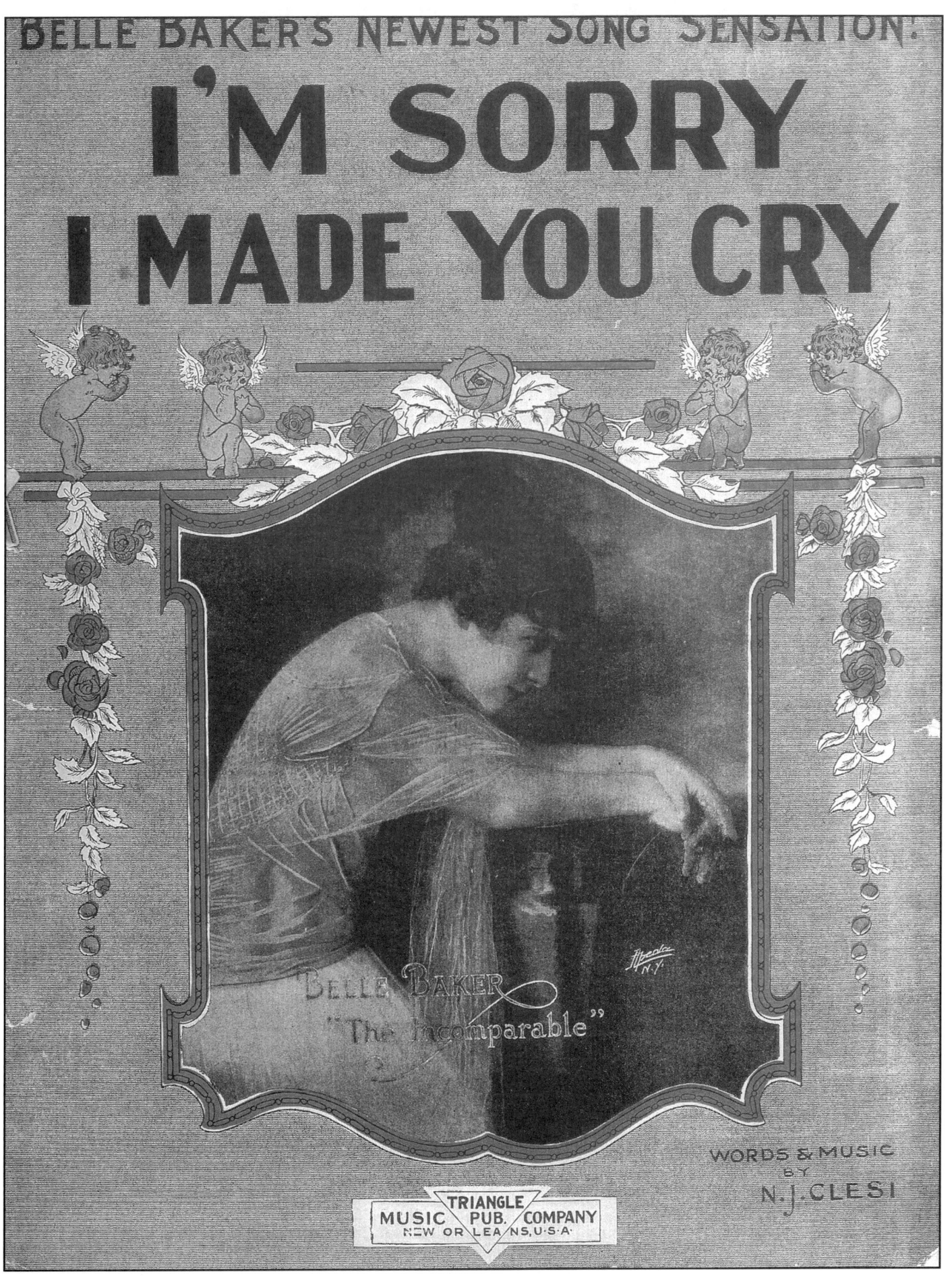

I'm Sorry I Made You Cry

By N.J. Clesi

1. Dear little girl have I made you sad?
   Your lips are trembling so!
   Those bitter tears will drive me mad,
   Jealous of me I know!
   Do you believe there's another girl,
   Do you believe me untrue?
   Tho' I have wandered in life's gay whirl,
   You've called me back to you.

2. Roses enrapture my thoughts with love,
   You are in ev'ry rose,
   And like the golden sun above,
   Your smile with heaven glows!
   My soul is thrill'd when the song birds sing,
   I hear your voice calling me!
   Come let us woo like the birds in spring,
   Oh, listen to my plea!

CHORUS: I'm sorry, dear, so sorry, dear,
I'm sorry I made you cry!
Won't you forget, won't you forgive?
Don't let us say goodbye!
One little word, one little smile,
One little kiss, won't you try?
It breaks my heart to hear you sigh,
I'm sorry I made you cry!

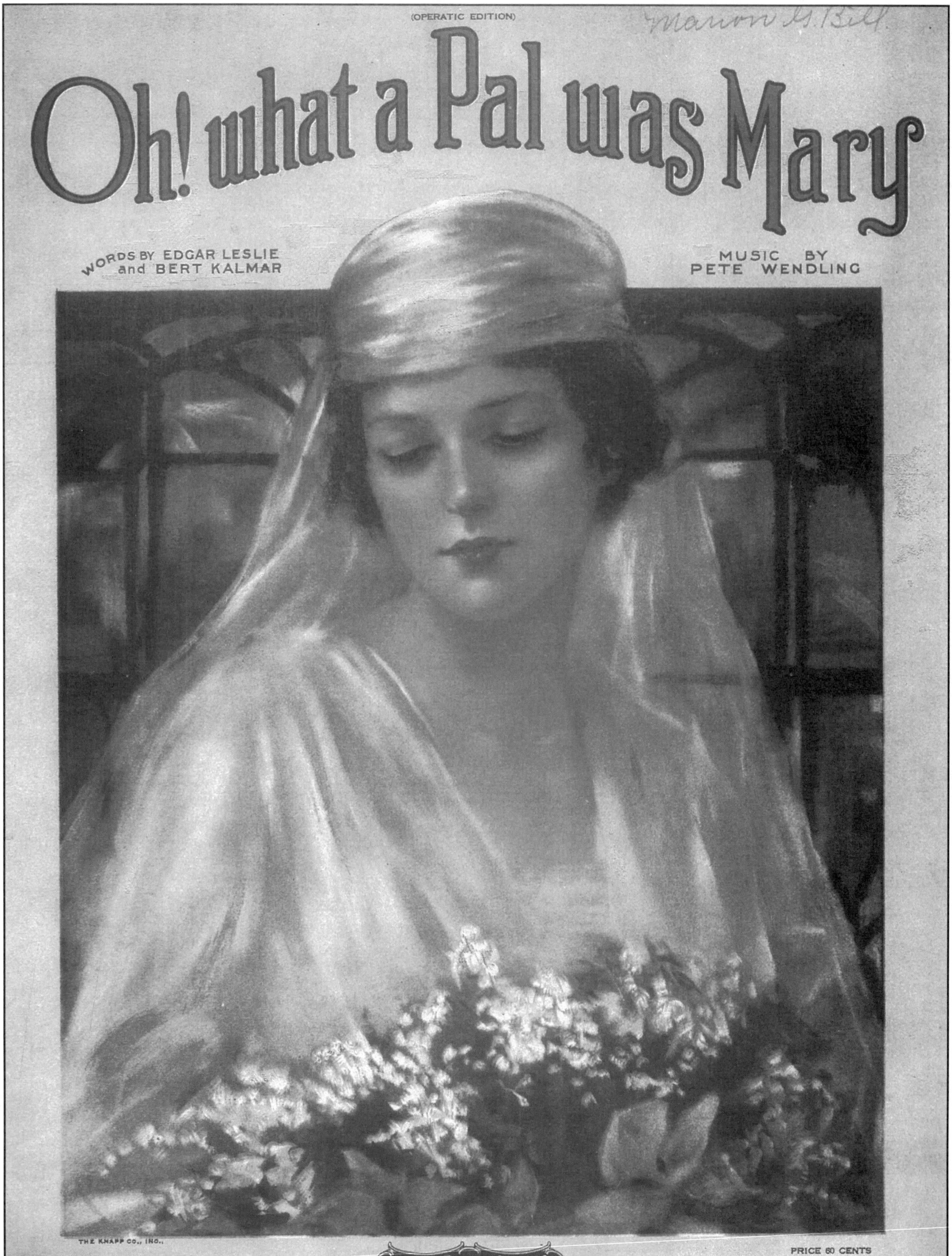

(OPERATIC EDITION)
Marion G. Bell
Oh! what a Pal was Mary
WORDS BY EDGAR LESLIE
and BERT KALMAR
MUSIC BY
PETE WENDLING
THE KNAPP CO., INC.
PRICE 60 CENTS
WATERSON-BERLIN & SNYDER CO.
STRAND BUILDING NEW YORK 47TH ST. & B'WAY

I'm Always Chasing Rainbows

Words by Joseph McCarthy

Music by Harry Carroll

1. At the end of the rainbow there's happiness,
   And to find it how often I've tried,
   But my life is a race, just a wild goose chase,
   And my dreams have all been denied.
   Why have I always been a failure.
   What can the reason be?
   I wonder if the world's to blame.
   I wonder if it could be me?

CHORUS: I'm always chasing rainbows,
Watching clouds drifting by.
My schemes are just like all my dreams,
Ending in the sky.
Some fellows look and find the sunshine,
I always look and find the rain.
Some fellows make a winning sometime,
I never even make a gain,
Believe me, I'm always chasing rainbows,
Waiting to find a little blue bird in vain.

I'm Forever Blowing Bubbles

By Jaan Kenbrovin
and
John William Kellette

62

1. I'm dreaming dreams
   I'm scheming schemes
   I'm building castles high
   They're born anew their days are few
   Just like sweet butterfly
   And as the daylight is dawning
   They come again in the morning.

2. When shadows creep
   When I'm asleep
   To lands of hope I stray
   Then at daybreak when I awake
   My bluebird flutters away.
   Happiness you seem so near me
   Happiness come forth and cheer me.

CHORUS: I'm forever blowing bubbles
Pretty bubbles in the air
They fly so high nearly reach the sky.
Then like my dreams they fade and die
Fortune's always hiding
I've looked ev'rywhere.
I'm forever blowing bubbles
Pretty bubbles in the air.

Blue Jeans

Words by Harry D. Kerr
Music by Lou Traveller

1. Back in the hills of the old Cumberland,
   Long, long ago there we strolled hand in hand;
   I called her Blue Jeans, a wild mountain rose,
   I wonder now if she knows I'm sighing

2. Spring time is here and the birds in the trees
   Still sing to me all the old melodies;
   Far down the trail I wander alone,
   But, old-en joys long have flown, Still I sing

CHORUS: Blue Jeans, the days are lonely,
   Blue Jeans, I dream of you,
   The wildwood May days and childhood play days,
   Those golden summer hours we knew;
   Songbirds are softly calling,
   Down where the grass is blue,
   The trail up yonder we used to wander,
   There, pretty Blue Jeans, I'll wait for you.

Homesick

1. I feel very blue, yes I do
   Can't you tell? Worry quite a lot
   'Cause I'm not feeling well
   Friends have come to me
   Saying, "We can see,
   You need company" but
   I'm not lonely, I'm only

2. My poor heart will stop when I hop
   Off the train, such a happy soul
   When I stroll down the lane
   I can't wait till then,
   To be there again,
   In the twilight when the
   Sun is setting I'm getting

CHORUS: Homesick, I know just what's the matter
I'm Homesick that's all,
I see that cosy little shack and the little red school,
Daddy on the back of a funny old mule
"God Bless our Home" on the wall
The fields of clover, they seem to say,
"Why don't you come over, pay us a call"
I miss the cows and the chickens and
The apple tree shady
And there's that little old lady
Do you wonder why I'm homesick?

*This page has been left
blank to avoid
awkward page turns*

The New Songs

When We're Dancing

Words and Music by
Ian Whitcomb

Copyright ©2000 by Ian Whitcomb Songs. Box 451, Altadena, CA 91003

1. When you step the light fantastic
you are quite a sight to see.
Yes, you do it so superbly
with every one but me!

CHORUS: When we're dancing — could you try to hold me close just sometimes?
When we're waltzing — could you try to make believe I'm there?
When we fox-trot — could you bounce a bit to show you mean it?
I'm only asking what I feel is fair.
When we tango — I am pretty sure of whom you're thinking.
When we lindy — I can see that old-time face in your eyes,
because I know him, my dear,
he's the man who yesteryear I used to be.
And that's the way that lovelight dies!

*This page has been left
blank to avoid
awkward page turns*

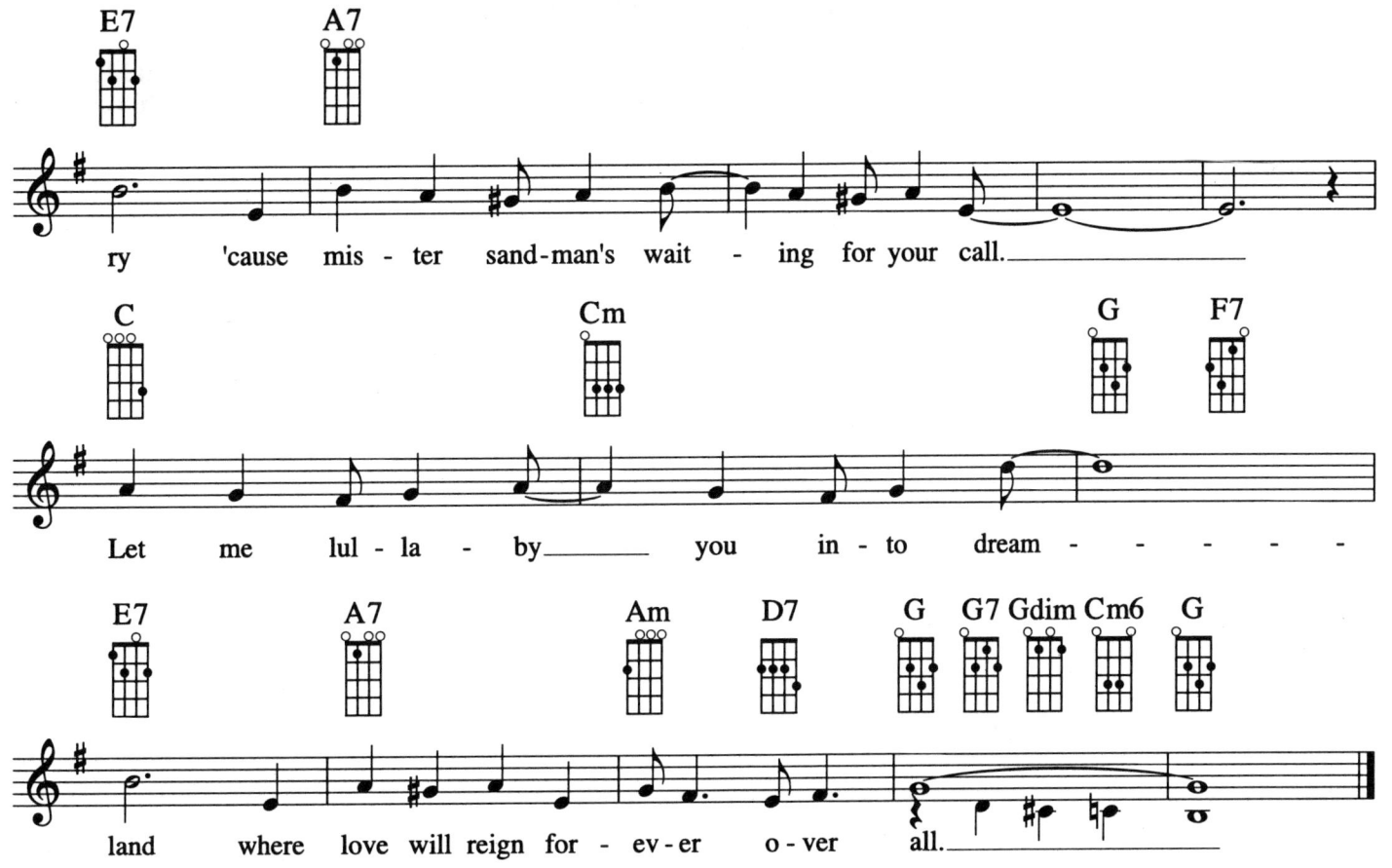

Dreams are what you need when you're unhappy.
Dreams will heal your heart when you are blue.
Just close your eyes — and picture sunny skies. —
Soon you'll be drifting into paradise — s'awful nice!
When the pain comes raining — don't you worry, —
'cause mister sandman's waiting for your call.
Let me lullaby you into dreamland
where love will reign forever over all.

If You've Ever Loved

Words and Music by
Ian Whitcomb

Copyright ©2000 by Ian Whitcomb Songs. Box 451, Altadena, CA 91003

If you've ever loved
You know it's worth it
'Spite of all the pain you know it's fine
'Tho they pass you by thinking
You're no-one
Stay up in the sky
Safe where you can shine
(So let them)
Leave you in the lurch
'Cos you've got something
They can never steal
—It's yours alone
'Tho she never cared
'Tho you never shared
The love that lit up your life
Don't lose that feeling sublime
—Keep it sharp as a knife!

I was one who lived alone and liked it.
But I never lacked a man or two.
Take a dinner here, take a movie there,
The tricky time was when the evening's through.
I sat list'ning to their pretty love tales.
Ev'ryone would sing the same refrain.
But I knew that words can sometimes turn to deeds;
Often I was left out in the rain.

They promised me a million rainbows.
They swore their love for me was true.
They said they'd see that all the pain goes.
They'd lead me where the skies are blue.
You didn't tell me any stories.
Your love refrains were fast and few.
You hardly said a thing and yet I heard bells ring.
You didn't say you loved me. I just knew.

On Paradise Island

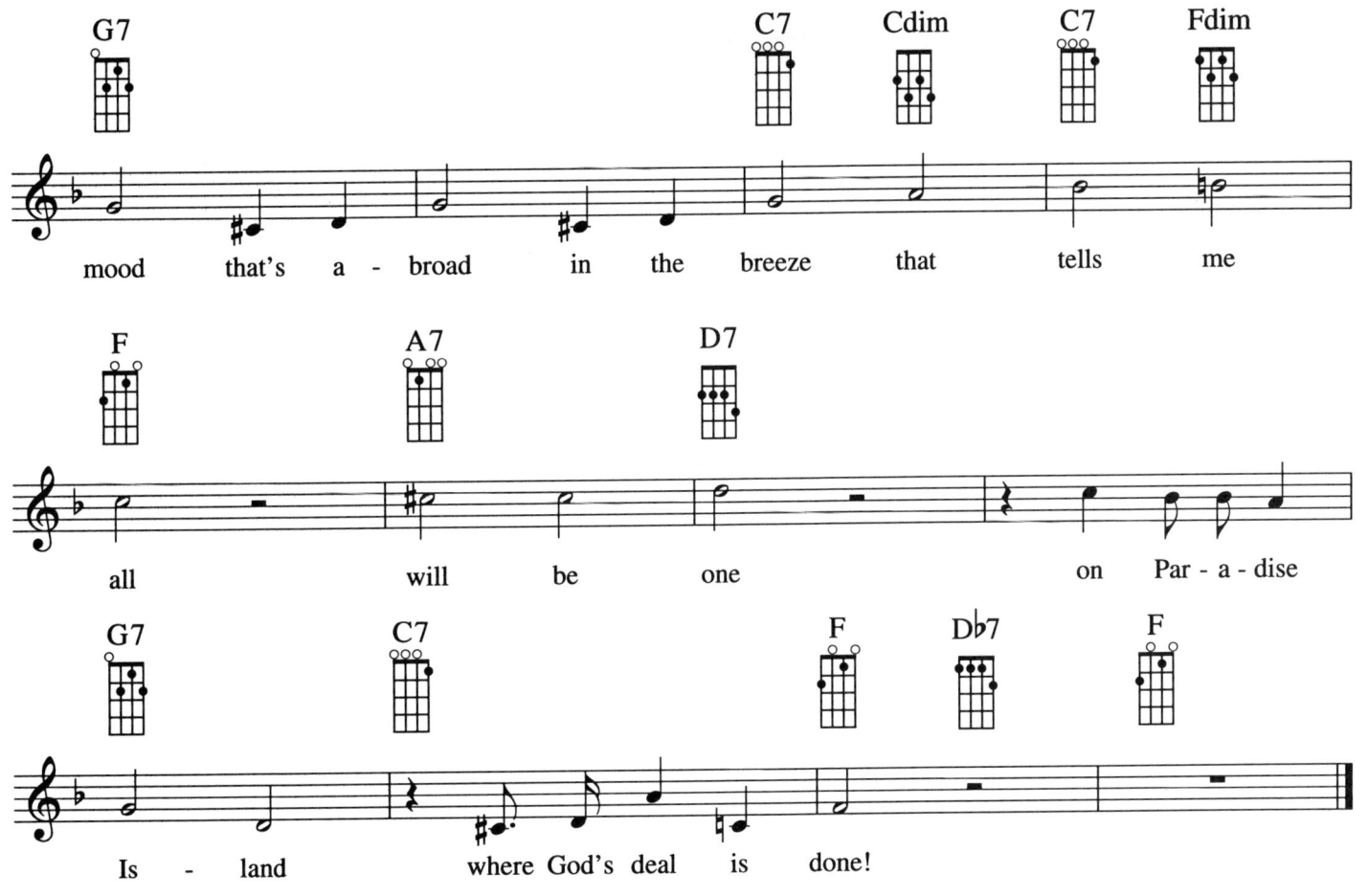

Please let me be—
On Paradise Island—
Far across the sea—
There I must stay—
For there is a quietude
Each and every day.
There's a tune in accord in the trees—
There's a mood that's abroad in the breeze
—That tells me—
All will be one
On Paradise Island
Where God's deal is done!

1. I walk the garden
   When day is done
   When things are quiet
   —No burning sun!
   I see the flowers
   I note the grass
   —Why can't the rain tumble down
   And bring sense to this mis'rable farce?

2. I pace the garden
   I must keep calm
   No need to panic
   No need for harm.
   I should feel healthy
   And show a smile
   —Instead I'm sinking so fast
   In a lake full of bubberling bile.

CHORUS: Why d'you go away?
—You know I can't live without you!
Ruining my day
—And making nighttime a hell!
I stroll the garden
—I'm now at peace
A precious moment of clarity
Then all my trouble will cease.

My Dog Has Fleas

Words and Music by
Ian Whitcomb

Copyright ©2000 by Ian Whitcomb Songs. Box 451, Altadena, CA 91003

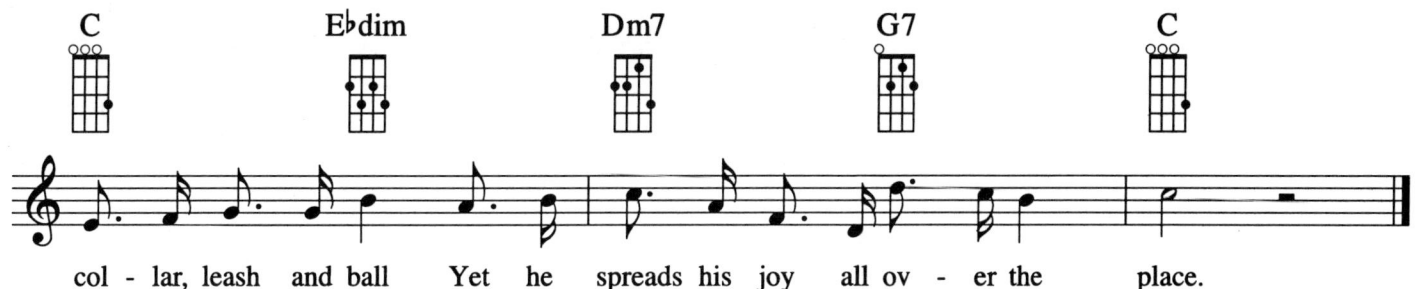

col - lar, leash and ball Yet he spreads his joy all ov - er the place.

My dog has fleas but he sprawls at his ease—
Letting sunlight and moonlight slide by him.
Glides down his stream in a wonderful dream—
Which I'd like to share
When I lie there beside him.
My life is rushed when it ought to be hushed
By the peace that I see in his face
He'll leave nothing much at all
But a collar, leash and ball
Yet he spreads his joy all over the place!

1. Thousands of love songs tell thousands of lies,
   Set in fabulous places 'neath ludicrous skies.
   But I've got a new song; don't call it a spoof.
   It's not too commercial, it's merely the truth.

CHORUS: You're my sweetheart, my wife and my mother.
You're the whole of my world rolled into one.
You sashay down the street like a lover,
But you're home when my day's work is done.
I confess I'm a fool to admit it,
But I guess I'm a boy right to the end.
Yet although you're my sweetheart, my wife and my "mum,"
You are also my very best friend!

I Love You

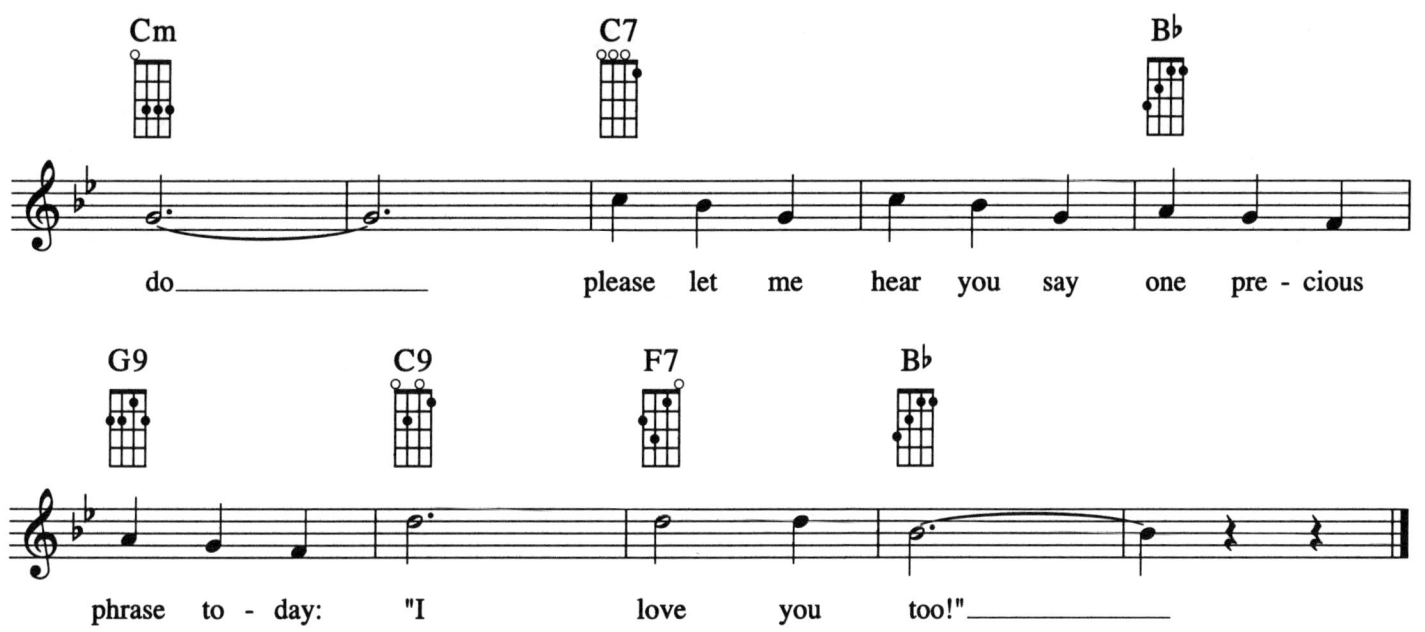

I love you,
Three little words so true
I could quote poems and make a big deal
But nothing expresses the way that I feel
Except "I love you."
But one little thing's left to do
Please let me hear you say
One precious phrase today:
"I love you too!"

Goodnight to you and see you once again.
I hope that you will miss me now and then.
I know the glow of your applause will burn,
But I hope that you got something in return.
Goodnight to you, God bless you one and all.
You make my life worthwhile.
And when the darkness turns to endless night,
I'll live forever after in your laughter and smiles.
We'll break the wall of darkness with your smiles.

Books By Ian Whitcomb

After The Ball: Pop Music from Rock to Rock (1972)
Tin Pan Alley: A Pictorial History (1975)
Lotusland: A Story of Southern California (1979)
Whole Lotta Shakin': A Rock 'n' Roll Scrapbook (1982)
Rock Odyssey: A Chronicle of the Sixties (1983)
Irving Berlin & Ragtime America (1987)
Resident Alien (1990)
The Beckoning Fairground: Notes of a British Exile (1994)
Treasures of Tin Pan Alley (1994)
Vaudeville Favorites (1995)
The Best Of Vintage Dance (1996)
Songs of the Ragtime Era (1997)
The Titanic Songbook (1998)
Titanic Tunes—Songs from Steerage (1998)
Songs of the Jazz Age (1998)
Ukulele Heaven (1999)